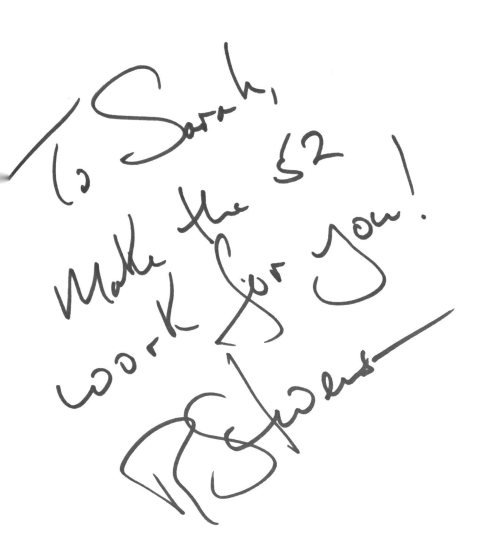

To Sarah,
To Make the 52
work for you!

52

Essential
Habits For Success

By
ROBERT STEVENSON

SEEKING EXCELLENCE PUBLISHING

Inquiries should be addressed to:

Permissions Department
Seeking Excellence Publishing
3078 Woodsong Lane, Clearwater, FL 33761

Library of Congress Control Number: 2008909233

52 Essential Habits For Success
By Robert Stevenson

ISBN   978-0-9654765-2-2

Seeking Excellence Publishing Company

Printed in the United States of America

2 3 4 5 6 7 8 9 10

www.robertstevenson.org

The book is dedicated to my son Tyler.
This all started as a project for me to share with him
what I felt were the essential rules he needed to follow to be successful.
The project turned into a book for us to share with the world.

A special thanks to my wife Ann
who was always happy to assist me
the countless times I asked the question,
"what do you think."

Acknowledgements

When I first started this project, I sent out an email to several of my friends and associates to get their thoughts on what they felt were the 10 most important habits a person should possess to be successful. Upon receiving their replies it became obvious, if you are planning on being successful, you will need to follow far more than 10 habits to get there.

It was reassuring to see there were some similarities in their responses such as integrity, goal setting, honesty, preparedness, optimism, and focus. But it was their different responses which pushed me to compile a more complete list. So, to Dennis Mandel, Andy Naples, Keith Kasen, Mona Meretsky, Bob Hannah, Mark Middleton, Joel Stevenson, Andrea Gold, and Donnie Mills, I would like to say thank you for participating in my endeavor to identify 52 Essential Habits for Success.

I compiled the list not only from my personal experiences and suggestions I received from the folks I just mentioned, but also from what I have learned from the hundreds of seminars I have attended, countless hours of listening to audio tracks from some of the greatest trainers of this century and the innumerable books, articles, magazines, newspapers and periodicals I have read. To all those great and talented people too numerous to list, thanks for sharing your wisdom.

Once I completed my first draft it was time to send it out to a few more of my friends, associates and family members to see what they thought of my book. I knew their criticisms would be fair and honest. I would like to thank Lisa Coleman, Christen Tonry, Dr. Mark Hepp, John Jennings, Brent League, Holly Davis, Sharon Yates, and my son Tyler for their honest assessments, candid feedback and helpful suggestions as to how I could make the book better.

It was time to let the skilled language technicians get involved in preparing my book for the public. I know from experience that I need a more qualified person than myself to proofread and edit my final manuscript. Lorraine Garrison, an English teacher extraordinaire, worked her magic in checking my spelling and grammar to prepare my book for final edit. Lori Donovan then exercised extraordinary talent in her meticulous review and edit of my final version. Thank you, ladies, for sharing your talent, knowledge, and experience.

I also need to thank the driving force behind this entire project, my son Tyler. I wanted to help him every way I could to shorten his learning curve in his journey towards reaching his full potential. Little did I know that he would be my best teacher. He has taught me to love more, give more, share more, forgive more, and enjoy life more. For all the obstacles that have been thrown at him in his life, he overcame them all and still came out smiling. He doesn't let anything keep him down. This book is but a small token of the payment I owe him for what he has done for me.

"For every disciplined effort there is a multiple reward."

Jim Rohn

Contents

"Sow a thought,
and you reap an act;

Sow an act,
and you reap a habit;

Sow a habit,
and you reap a character;

Sow a character,
and you reap a destiny."

Charles Reade

To Maximize the Effectiveness of This Book
YOU MUST FOLLOW
THESE CRITICAL INSTRUCTIONS

Why is it that some people succeed while others fail or lead lives of mediocrity? Now, I'm not suggesting a life of mediocrity is bad. If that is your aspiration, then so be it. But if you aspire to be something more, then you need the answer to this question: **What do you need to do to be successful?** That answer seems to elude most people. I have written this book to address that specific question.

Give me the amount of time it takes to brush your teeth in the morning and evening, just that amount of time, no more, and I will show you a way to substantially improve your level of success.

I have read some excellent books which addressed the topic of success in great detail. Many of them have had some outstanding suggestions of what one should do to be successful. I personally think one of the things wrong with most self-help books is they are just too difficult to implement. In most cases, after a person reads a self-help book, they appreciate the wisdom of the author, and have every intention of following through on the suggestions the author made. The problem is they just get burdened down with all the steps they must take, things they must do, lists they must write, and self-analysis they must ponder to help them become a better person. Even those who have really good intentions find it extremely difficult to stick to the plan the author has laid out in the book. Their intentions were good. They actually finished reading the book, but they became overwhelmed with all the things the author said "*they must do*" if they are to become successful. So instead of mapping out a total plan of action you probably won't adhere to, I felt it better to make some critical visual impressions that will help you see your way to becoming a much more talented, motivated, productive, and successful individual.

Most people don't like to study, refer back to books or articles they read, prepare lists, or assess their current situation and then change the way they do certain things. So how can I get you to replace old, unhelpful, sometimes destructive wasteful habits with new, helpful, useful habits without having you do all the things I just mentioned?

I have designed a simple way for you to condition your mind with powerful success habits that when used will be the driving force behind your future success. Many of you reading this book are already successful and are looking for more ways to maintain that success. This book will be helpful for you as well. The success habits I will be sharing are universal, easy to understand, but most importantly, effective. The method I will be using to introduce (or re-introduce) these habits for success is about as simple as it gets. *The problem with the simplicity of this program is most people will have a tendency to move ahead at a faster pace; please don't. The structure of the program, not just the habits, is what helps to give it such power and effectiveness.*

Psychologists have suggested if you see, read, or do something 14-21 times, it becomes a part of you. I am going to be a little more specific and say you can develop a habit with 14 specific encounters as long as your intention (frame of mind) is such that you are truly trying to accomplish the task, rather than just going through the motions. I plan to instill 52 essential habits into your mind with no major studying, practicing, drilling or rehearsing. In fact, it will be done pretty effortlessly if you will follow one simple set of instructions.

After reading my "Critical Instructions" on how to maximize the effectiveness of this book, you will find 52 habits for success, each on a perforated page, designed so you can tear each one out of the book and tape it on your bathroom mirror. The simple objective is for you to read the one habit every morning and evening for one week, when you are in the bathroom brushing your teeth. It is that simple:

TEAR IT OUT
TAPE IT UP
READ IT TWICE PER DAY FOR SEVEN DAYS
GO GET THE NEXT ONE AND DO IT AGAIN

(By the way – you don't have to worry about saving the pages you have torn out of the book, because I have a second copy in the book for you.)

The reason why this program will be so effective is because you will be involving both your conscious and subconscious mind in establishing the habits you need to incorporate into your daily life if you are going to be truly successful. You see, after you read the success habit with your conscious mind, your subconscious mind will then take over. Your subconscious mind will start thinking about this one simple success habit all day long until it becomes a part of you. You will begin to know it, you will understand it, and subconsciously you will start to do it. Before long, these 52 habits will be permanently conditioned in your mind, to help lead you on your journey to an extremely successful life.

Don't try and shorten the learning curve by only reading each success habit for one, two, or three days, thinking you can obtain your desired goal sooner if you were to only shorten the amount of time you spend on each habit. Nothing worth having was ever accomplished well by taking a shortcut.

You are probably thinking right now,
***it is going to take me one full year to get through this book;
that's ridiculous.***

First of all, you are right. Yes, it will take you one full year to get through this entire book, if you want to get the full impact of the program. But you need to understand, it does not take one full year for you to start reaping the benefits of what the book teaches. Once you get started, your subconscious mind starts taking advantage of what you have already read as you progress through the 52 success habits. By the time you have completed going through all the habits, you will already be well on your way to being extremely successful; reaping the substantial rewards that will come with it as you progress through the book.

You will notice a huge difference in your life after only the first month. Just allow yourself to read, receive, believe, and you will start achieving. It is a proven fact what you read can affect your thoughts and actions, so I am merely going to affect them in a positive way. **Everything you will ever be is totally up to you.** You are where you are today because of your past decisions, and your future is completely in your hands. These success habits will help you make better decisions. Let them work for you. If you will take the time to absorb the habits, you will change your life for the better.

If what you have been doing isn't working, or it's not working as well as you would like it to, then what have you got to lose? Taking a couple of minutes twice per day to read something taped to your mirror isn't much time to give up. I think I can safely say most people wouldn't classify their teeth brushing time as their most thought provoking or productive moments of their day. The key element to making this work for you, are the 14 repetitions and then having your subconscious mind kicking in after each reading. According to Peter Ouspensky in his book *In Search of the Miraculous,* he estimated that the subconscious mind functions at almost thirty thousand times the speed of our conscious mind. We are going to use this power to your benefit. It has been proven your subconscious mind will believe whatever your conscious mind tells it, without question. Your subconscious mind will start working on this "input" to try and make it become a reality. This is the power you need to harness for yourself. **A power that can work thirty thousand times faster is something you need to take advantage of.**

I implore you not to read ahead. You need to let your subconscious mind help you in becoming successful. To become a medical doctor, in most cases you have to study another four years after college. To become a specialist, you would have to study even more. The effort put forth to earn a medical degree is enormous. I am not asking you to put forth that kind of effort and time. I am simply asking for a few minutes each day for 52 weeks to identify, teach, and then instill in you these necessary habits of success. Anything worthwhile takes time. **It's your life and you have only got one shot at it; this isn't a dress rehearsal.** When it is over, you don't get a redo. So follow my plan and reap the benefits. It's your choice.

Before we get started with identifying and establishing the powerful success habits which will be the driving force behind your future success, I need you to admit to something. **You must accept, without any reluctance, you are where you are today because of you and the choices you have made.** You can only start to mature and grow when you finally accept there is no one out there who is going to save you. Your slogan for success from this point forward is simply …

"If it is to be, it's up to me."

Socrates was once asked by a young man how he could gain wisdom. Socrates asked the young man to accompany him while he took a stroll around a lake and he would discuss the matter with him. Socrates then asked the lad to follow him into the lake where they were standing in water that was chest deep. This seemed odd to the young man, but who was he to question Socrates. Then all of a sudden, Socrates grabbed the young man and pushed him down until his head was fully submerged under the water and held him there. At first, the young man thought this was just a joke, so he didn't fight back. Socrates held him longer and longer until the lad panicked and started struggling to free himself from Socrates' grasp. He was running out of air, his lungs were aching for oxygen, his heart was pounding, and his adrenalin was sky-high.

Socrates finally released his grasp so the young man could emerge. Grasping for air, panic-stricken from the ordeal, the young man screamed out in a barely audible voice, *"What are you doing?"* Socrates calmly replied, *"When you desire wisdom with the same intensity that you desired to breathe, then nothing will stop you from getting it."*

I can share with you the wisdom of the 52 habits. I can put them in a format that will help make them a part of your daily life. But until you have the burning desire to learn, change, adapt, and commit to them, this will only be a futile exercise. Let me put a little twist to Socrates' quote:

"When you desire to become successful with the same intensity that you desire to breathe, then nothing will stop you."

Now, let's get started.

Here are your
52 Essential Habits For Success

…Remember…
Don't rush ahead and read them all.

For this learning system to be effective, you need to
concentrate on only one habit per week.

So tear out your first **"Habit"** along the perforation,
and go tape it to your mirror.

Let's get started!

Habit #1
Believe in Yourself

If you don't believe in yourself, why should anyone else believe in you? Sure you are going to make mistakes; that is part of life. People want to be around confident people. One of the most important traits of any leader is their confidence in themselves. People don't want to follow someone who lacks self-confidence. When you first start out, you may have to *fake it before you make it;* that is okay. All of us at one time in our lives were young and inexperienced. None of us were born with all the knowledge, experience and talents we would need to be successful. These are all developed skills. So relax and learn from your mistakes, realizing we have all passed this way before. Have the confidence to tell yourself you will get it, learn it, or figure it out. It might take you a while, but realize you know you have what it takes to do it. Start believing in yourself, and others will start believing in you, too.

Habit #2
Act as if the World is Watching

Thomas Jefferson said, *"Whenever you are to do a thing, though it can never be known but to yourself, ask yourself how you would act were the world looking at you, and act accordingly."* Even though that was said over 200 years ago, it is still great advice for today, especially in this technological world with people carrying mini video-recorders in their cell phones. The next thing you know, your actions are being shown on national TV or on the Internet for all the world to see. So act as if there is a camera on you at all times and act accordingly. The great philosopher Seneca said,

> *"I will govern my life and thoughts as if the whole world were to see the one and to read the other."*

Habit #3
Practice, Drill & Rehearse, Then Take the Initiative

If you want to beat your competition, then you have to be willing to put in the time to *practice, drill, and rehearse* (PDR). The great ones don't need someone telling them to practice. They understand when they are not practicing, someone else is, and when they meet that person on the field of competition, that person will win. Success comes to those who take the initiative to do more, stay longer, and work harder. The day you understand your success is dependent on you - *your own desire, initiative, and fortitude* - is the day you start achieving greatness. To the great ones, PDR is not a motto on some wall, it is a way of life. Simply stated:

If you want to be the best at what you do, then practice more than the rest, and success will come to you.

Habit #4
Don't be Afraid to Fail

It's amazing how much experience can be gained by making a mistake. As Henry Ford once stated: *"Failure is the opportunity to begin again more intelligently."* If you never try to do something beyond what you already know how to do, you will never get any better. Failure is a major component to your success process. You didn't learn to walk after your first try, or feed yourself, talk, ride a bike, or play a musical instrument. There were a multitude of attempts before you became proficient at any of these. Notice, I said attempts, not failures. You need to decide that *there are no failures in life, only results.* Failure isn't fatal unless you quit. If you didn't like the results, then analyze what went wrong, learn, and then alter your method. The failed attempt will merely teach you that your method was flawed; so correct it and try again. Failure is something that happens to you; it's an event, not a person.

Habit #5
Make Goal Setting a Habit

If you don't know where you are going, then how will you know when you get there? The vast majority of people don't set goals, and the vast majority of people do not reach their full potential, thus limiting their level of success. I think you will find a correlation there. You have got to decide what it is you want and **write it down;** some call it "thinking on paper". You then have to decide what it is you will have to do to make what you have written down become a reality. The first two steps in making a dream become a reality are to write it down and then set a deadline. Remember to be "SMART" about your goals: *Specific, Measurable, Attainable, Realistic, and Timely.* Determining your goals will determine your actions which, when accomplished, will determine your success. It has been proven that people with goals earn twice as much as those without goals. Being successful starts with establishing your goals.

Habit #6
You Must Pay the Price

One of the most valuable things you possess is your willpower. Great accomplishments come from great efforts. You will have to pay a price if you are to be successful. Hard work, practice, patience, sacrifice, and rehearsing are all words **Super Achievers** understand. The question is: are you willing to **Pay the Price** for greatness? What you say, what you wish for, and what you hope for doesn't count. Your actions are all that matter. Your actions are the only thing that will get you success. The price of mediocrity is far less than the price of greatness. It is easier to settle for being average than to strive for greatness. The choice is yours and yours alone.

Habit #7
Never, Never, Never Give Up

Elbert Hubbard captures the point I am trying to make so profoundly in his words: *"There is no defeat except in no longer trying. There is no defeat save within ..."* Failure is just a result in the learning process; giving up is a choice. Walt Disney was fired for lack of creativity and went bankrupt twice before he was able to turn his dream into a reality. At one time Donald Trump had a negative net worth of $900 million. Most people would have declared bankruptcy. Seven years later he was worth over $2 billion. It took Ray Kroc, founder of McDonald's, twenty-seven years to make his first million. Bill Gates' first Microsoft company went bankrupt. He then became the richest man in the world. Giving up is a choice, a very bad choice.

Habit # 8
Hang Out with Successful People

If you want to be successful, then you need to "hang out" with successful people. Watch what they do and how they work at their chosen profession. Unconsciously, you will start adapting these behaviors, habits, attitudes, and opinions of these successful individuals. Dr. David McClelland of Harvard found, after twenty-five years of research, that the choice of a "negative reference group" is enough to condemn a person to failure and underachievement in life. The good doctor simply means, ***if you hang out with people who are going nowhere with their lives, then you'll be headed in that same direction.*** If you can't be around successful people, then read as many biographies/autobiographies as you can about successful people. Personally, I would rather be by myself than with people who are headed nowhere. What will you choose?

Habit # 9
Success Requires Self-Discipline

Self-discipline is making yourself do what you need to do when you need to do it whether you want to or not. In the overall scheme of success, being self-disciplined is the most important trait you must possess. You can know, understand, and identify what must be done, but if you don't have the discipline to do it, it's all for naught. The true test of your character lies in your self-discipline. Your persistence to make things happen, your resolve, and your willpower will determine just how successful you will be in life. There will be days you won't feel like getting up and doing what needs to be done. Those are the days your character is being tested. The great ones get it done regardless of how they feel. Remember your action statement:

If it is to be, it's up to me.

Habit #10
Accept Criticism
for the Benefits it Brings

There is nothing fun about receiving criticism. It is amazing how painful words can be if we let them. It was once said: **"There is nothing either good or bad but thinking makes it so."** So channel the criticizing words differently. Regardless of the agenda of the person giving the criticism, use the words to your betterment even if they were given for someone else's gain. This is all about creating a better you, not a better them. Filter out all pain and prejudice and allow only the things that will benefit you to enter your mind. Dr. Norman Vincent Peale stated: *"The trouble with most of us is that we would rather be ruined with praise than saved with criticism."* Sometimes the only way you are going to know if you are doing something wrong is by someone telling you. Criticism is therefore helpful and should be accepted in that manner.

Habit #11
Contain Your Anger

Anger is a self–induced reaction to an external stimulus. In other words, something happened that you didn't like, and you got angry. Outbursts of anger can cause stress, heart attacks, ulcers, headaches, lack of control, saying things we don't mean, fights, and retaliations, all of which are bad. The amazing thing about anger is that it is unnecessary. Anger comes from within you. It is a response you choose to give when you feel you are being victimized, treated unfairly, cheated, or taken advantage of. The next time you feel your anger raising up its ugly head, take a moment and get control, making certain that you don't say a word. Remember, the person screaming in an argument is the person losing the argument. You can respond in an angry manner or a calm one. Anger is a choice, not a cause or condition.

Habit #12
Smile - It's Good for You and Those Around You

There are thousands of languages we don't understand, but yet a smile is understood no matter what language is being spoken. To successfully deal with people, you need to create trust, confidence, and rapport. It is a proven fact that the simple physical response of a smile will help to create all three. If you want to be more successful, have less stress, more friends, and better health, then smile more. Smiling is good for you, and it's good for the people around you. Make it a habit to smile when you are greeting anyone. When you are asking someone for help, smile. If you want to change your negative state of mind, smile. People want to be around people who are in good moods, and being in a good mood all starts with a smile. Smiling displays your frame of mind and warmth without having to say a word, and it puts you in a positive mood; this is all good.

Habit #13
Look for Ways to Praise Often

If you want to have a lot of friends in business and in your personal life, then look for ways to compliment *(praise)* them often. Make sure it is sincere praise and not contrived. Think how great you feel when someone tells you that you did a good job. Complimenting someone is not a hard thing to do, but we seem to forget to do it, even when the perfect opportunity avails itself. If you make it a habit to praise people rather than condemn, you will be amazed how many people will want to help you. Making people feel good about themselves will never do you any harm. On the contrary, it will do nothing but good for you. There is an old saying that will benefit you greatly if you utilize it. *You can get whatever you want if you help other people get what they want.* Go out of your way to compliment people, and your journey to success will become easier.

Habit #14
Shorten Your Learning Curve by Reading

Life is too short for you to learn all there is to know by personal experience. Reading is an excellent way to shorten your learning curve. The gifts of knowledge, insight, wisdom, and experience can all be bestowed upon you if you will merely take the time to read what brilliant people have written. The great self-help and inspirational author Og Mandino once wrote, *"the only difference in you now and you five years from now, are the people you meet and the things that you read."* I would take heed to his words. Reading will improve your creativity, vocabulary, spelling, and language skills. Make it a part of your daily routine to read something (*at least five days per week*) that will help you become a better person, spouse, friend, associate, parent, athlete, student, employee, and/or boss. Becoming a smarter person is only a book away.

Habit #15
Never Neglect Your Body

When you neglect your body, your energy levels diminish, fatigue sets in, and illness ensues. Exercise is a key factor in all aspects of your success. There is a litany of incredible benefits to your overall health if you maintain a proper exercise program. Physical activity reduces stress, increases energy, gives you greater stamina, helps manage your weight, improves muscle tone, aids in digestion, helps you relax, clears your mind, gives you a better outlook on life (more positive and optimistic), enhances your sexual response, increases alertness, improves sleep, and may possibly reduce your need for certain medications. So get up and get moving with some kind of structured exercise program a minimum of three times per week. Remember, *if you don't use it, you will lose it.*

Habit #16

Be Positive
It's the Only Way to Act

Being negative causes stress, illness, worry, anger, reduces productivity, takes the fun out of life, and makes others not want to be around you. You are going to have bad days, equipment failures, traffic congestion, delays, spills, mistakes, misunderstandings, dealings with jerks and idiots, car problems, and unexpected expenses (to name just a few) in your life. The remarkable thing about life is every moment we have a choice regarding the attitude we embrace. If I have the choice, I would rather be around a positive person than a negative one. Olympic gold medalist figure skater Scott Hamilton stated, ***"the only disability in life is a bad attitude."*** It doesn't mean bad things don't happen to positive people. It just means positive people don't let bad things hold them back. Having a positive attitude doesn't guarantee your success, but it's a great place to start.

Habit #17
Watch What You Say

Remember what Jefferson said in Habit #2, "... *act were the world looking at you, and act accordingly.*" Things have a way of coming back to haunt you. People take things out of context to support their own personal agenda. I think the best rule to follow is to say nothing about anyone you wouldn't have the courage to say directly to their face. Stick to what you know to be factual, not on hearsay or rumor. Someday you may have to defend your comments, so make sure you speak only the truth. Most of the problems you will encounter in your life are people problems. Most of those problems stem from what someone said or did. So select your words wisely, positively, and according to facts, because having to eat them later is not a pleasurable experience.

Habit #18

Want an Advantage – Be Early

If you want to reduce your stress, then be early. If you want to impress your boss, coach, or teacher, then be early. Being late shows a lack of respect for whomever you're dealing with. I'm not talking about going to a party and being the first one there. We'll have to deal with the proper social etiquette at another time. I am talking about virtually everything else. Staying ahead of the game, ahead of the deadline, ahead of when you have to be somewhere, and ahead of when the project is due will forever endear you to those who are expecting anything on time. Being early shows others you are motivated, organized, and disciplined. Be known as the one they can always count on to be early, prepared, and excited to be there, and you will have everyone wanting you on their team. True leaders don't keep people waiting.

Habit #19

Do More Than Expected

If you want to position yourself for success, then always do more than expected. By incorporating this one single habit into everything you do, you will basically be guaranteeing your success in life. The people who do the minimum required will usually get the minimum return. All great athletes, musicians, actors, lawyers, doctors, business people, etc., etc., understand for them to excel at their profession, they have to be willing to do more than those around them. You will never become an exceptional athlete by practicing the bare minimum. The great ones are forever practicing, working out, and studying their sport more than their competition. Whatever the task, do more than expected, and I can assure you your life will turn out better than you expected.

Habit #20
Say "Thank You" Often

Two of the most powerful words in the English language are *"thank you."* These two words are so simple to say, but so seldom used. You can carry it even further with words such as: *"I really appreciate that." "You were so kind to help me." "I couldn't have done this without you." "You were such a big help to me."* We get so caught up in the speed of our daily lives that we forget to say the words that will help make people want to assist us again. Regardless of your position or status in life, you should never forget to say these two words. When someone lets you cut in a line of traffic and they can't hear the words, you can still mouth them so they see that you are saying "thank you." Some people would simply call this common courtesy; I call it required courtesy for a successful life.

Habit #21

Remember People's Names

The words that are most familiar to you and the least threatening are the words that make up your name. If you want to get someone to relax, make yourself seem more acceptable to them, present yourself as less intimidating, then start or finish your opening statement to them by incorporating their name into the sentence. When you first meet someone, try saying their name several times while you are speaking to them so it will help you better remember their name when they leave. People will be extremely impressed if you have just met them and you remember their name the next time you see them. It is a sure way of showing your respect to them by proving their name was important enough for you to remember it.

Habit #22
Let Them Know You Care

There is enormous power in sending cards, notes, or letters to people. Using the Internet to stay in touch with friends, associates, and clients is helpful, but if you want to stand out from the rest of the crowd, send them something they don't have to print off on their printer. If you want to really stand out, remember people on special occasions, holidays, and especially their birthday. Former President George H.W. Bush used to spend two hours every night writing notes to friends, family, and acquaintances. People will appreciate the fact that you went to the trouble to not only remember them, but also took the time to handwrite a simple message. Putting that message in a nice card would be even better. Always remember, ***people don't care how much you know until they know how much you care.***

Habit #23
Always Use Good Manners

In this fast-paced techno-gadget world where people text rather than talk, e-mail rather than converse, and hurry rather than help, **a person who shows a little common courtesy will be the exception rather than the norm.** Opening doors for folks, pulling out chairs, letting someone else go first, waiting for everyone to be served before you start eating are all just simple, courteous gestures, but they say volumes about the type of person you are. These gestures are not just for the special people; they are for everyone. I don't like to be around people who are rude, arrogant, loud, and obnoxious or who don't have the decency to treat everyone with proper respect, regardless of their socioeconomic status. Treat everyone as if they were your equal, and always **shower them with courtesy and good manners.**

Habit #24
Beware of Fads

Fads come and go. The problem with that statement is that they go. The desire to stay up with the latest fashion trends, wear the "right" clothes or tattoo, drive the "hot" car, have the latest cell phone or technological gadget isn't new. It was that way 50 years ago, and it will be the same 50 years from now. I am not going to address what makes people "cool." My concern comes when a fad has something to do with permanently altering your body. The tattoo you love today, you may hate ten years from now. When it comes to doing permanent things to your body such as tattoos, piercing, and brands, I would suggest you give it serious thought and never do it on a whim or a dare. Permanent is a big commitment to something that may not be "cool" later on in your life. You can buy new cars and clothes and get rid of the old ones, but permanent is forever.

Habit #25

Pay Attention to Your First Impression

You will never get a second chance to make a good first impression, so that first impression really matters. You want the way you look to demand respect. People like to deal with individuals who are successful, and that means you need to look the part. I always feel if a person doesn't respect their own appearance, then what other things do they have little respect for? It doesn't take a huge income to be clean and well-groomed with clothes pressed and shoes polished. I will be grading you the moment you walk in the door, so get my attention by paying attention to yourself. Companies don't want an unkempt, disheveled, messy, uncombed person representing them. A critical part of being professional is looking professional. If you want someone to pay attention to you, then you must first pay attention to yourself.

Habit #26
Prepare Now or Fail Later

The great college basketball coach John Wooden (who won 88 consecutive games, 11 NCAA national championships, 7 of them in a row) had a saying: *"Failure to prepare is preparing to fail."* The truly successful people leave nothing to chance. They put in the time, effort, research, and thought to ensure they will achieve their desired goal. You don't climb Mount Everest by showing up with some climbing gear and start to climb. You spend months planning out the entire journey, day by day, moment by moment. This is your life and you've got one shot at it. All success begins with a definite purpose, a specific objective, and a plan to achieve it. It's your choice; *prepare now or fail later.*

Habit #27
Show Excitement in Your Greetings

I have never seen a dog, when its master walks in the door, turn its head and say *"Yo! I had a bad day. Not enough water, not enough dog food, you didn't leave the air conditioner on 72°, and the cat has got to go."* A dog is always happy to see its master. The tail is wagging; it's jumping around acting like it hasn't seen its master in months. A dog doesn't do it some of the time; it does it all the time. What a great feeling the dog gives to its master. The simple expression of *I am really happy to see you* makes anyone feel good. I am not telling you to jump around and look foolish every time you see someone. But I am suggesting you get up, make eye contact, give them a smile, and show a genuine interest in them. You will find that people will love to be around you, look forward to seeing you, and include you in their plans, parties, and get-togethers. People love dogs because dogs love people, and they show it. The key words are, "they show it" **every time**.

Habit #28
Be Persistent, Relentless, Determined

What will separate you from those average souls out there who stay mired in mediocrity will be your willpower, your desire to see it through, to not fail, to pay the price to achieve success. Always think your next great victory is just about to happen. Thomas Edison failed over 11,000 times trying to invent the light bulb. A person one time asked him what it felt like failing over 11,000 times. Mr. Edison said, *"I didn't fail 11,000 times. I discovered 11,000 ways how not to do it."* Some of the greatest success stories ever written are about people who overcame incredible adversities, obstacles, and/or rejections. They just kept working at it, refining their skills, or changing their methods until they made it. The difference between average and great starts with relentlessly applying all your physical and mental talents **to one task at a time** until you have completed the task.

Habit #29
Search Out Role Models

In most cases, you aren't the first person to ever attempt your chosen goal. If you want to be great at your chosen profession, remember, others have passed this way before you who have learned great lessons they would love to share. You might not be able to talk to Michael Jordan one on one, but you can read about his life and how he became an incredible basketball player. In many cases, there are people who would love to share the lessons they have learned if you just ask them. People love a compliment. Approaching someone and asking for their help because you respect what they have accomplished and would like to learn from them is a great compliment to them. Remember, to receive help you have to ask for help.

Habit #30
Never Waste Time

When you are wasting your time, you are wasting your life. Your life is a finite amount of time made up of moments. Each moment, second, minute, hour, day that passes can never be relived or re-captured. Why would you waste a limited resource, an irreplaceable commodity that you can never get back? Successful people take full advantage of their time. They plan their day ahead of time. Time management skills are an essential tool for anyone who wants to be successful. You can do nothing about the time you have already lost, but you can do everything with the time you have left. **Every minute spent in planning your day saves about ten minutes in executing it.** If you are to accomplish your goals, then you will need to be productive and efficient with your time management. If you are not planning your day, then your day will be planning you.

Habit #31
Always Be Truthful

The truth is but a simple thing, for it knows no right or
wrong. There are those who would alter it
to make the truth be gone.

They will speak, imply, suggest what you know are not
the facts. But the truth will remain the same,
rest assured it will be back.

It may be for the moment, the truth is not revealed.
There you stand betrayed by one,
accused of what's not real.

But for those of us who have been wronged,
take solace in what I say.
There will come a time where all will know
in some uncertain way.

The truth will rise above it all and prove their words
were wrong, causing those who spoke the words,
reputations now be gone.

The truth is but a simple thing, it may be hard to say.
The truth is but a simple thing,
and for me the only way.

Habit #32
Don't Gossip – It's a Waste of Time

What do you accomplish when you gossip about other people? Nothing, except wasting time. You haven't learned a thing, you have helped no one, and you have accomplished nothing. I hate to use such a simple adage, but I can think of no other way to say it better. **If you can't say something nice about someone, then don't say it.** Don't get yourself caught up in the bashing, trashing, smashing, gossiping conversations. By wasting your precious time in this common activity, you are really hurting yourself. Why would you ever want to do that? We have already established the importance of not wasting time, and gossiping is a huge time waster. *Always ask yourself … is what I am doing now taking me closer to where it is I want to go?* If the answer is no, then stop what you are doing and get back on track.

Habit #33

Concentrate on
Your Strengths & Interests

When you focus most of your time and energy on things you are good at, you will reap enormous rewards. Sometimes your strengths will be hidden in your interests. Don't try to be something your physical or mental abilities won't allow you to be. Focus on what you can do rather than on things you can't. If you aren't certain where your strengths lie, then focus on things you enjoy doing rather than on things you hate. Couple your interests with your strengths, and then commit to concentrated practice and study. Your concerted efforts will reap you enormous rewards, and you will also enjoy your journey towards success.

Habit #34
Become Interested in Others

Shakespeare wrote, *"The fragrance of a rose lingers on the hand that casts it."* Bestowing positive sentiments on or about others will eventually find a way back to you. Talk to people about what interests them, not you, and listen attentively. Getting people to talk about their favorite subject (themselves) is easy. Just start asking questions. To paraphrase Kipling, *"six honest serving men taught me all I knew; their names were What, Why, When, How, Where and Who."* Your objective in any conversation is to be listening more than you are speaking. Try and resist complaining about or criticizing others. By showing appreciation and admiration, by being agreeable and accepting, you will be a welcomed participant in any conversation. Being interested in others makes them more interested in you.

Habit #35
Expand Your Vocabulary

There are over 650,000 words in the English language. The average person knows about 15,000 and a child of 5 knows about 5,000. A very scary statistic is that after the age of 30, the average person learns about 5 words per year. If we live to be 75 years old, this would mean a person currently 30 years of age will learn an additional 225 words the rest of their life. If you want to set yourself apart from the masses, start with learning one new word per week. That would mean a 30-year-old person would learn an additional 2,340 words over the rest of their life rather than a paltry 225. The use of an excellent vocabulary will distinguish you from others and is usually an excellent indicator you are an intelligent person. So if you want to appear smart, then work on expanding your vocabulary.

Habit #36
Don't Cheat the Face in the Glass

Below is a poem by an unknown author I have taken the liberty to paraphrase. I feel it best addresses **Cheating Yourself.**

When you get what you want
in your struggle for self
and the world makes you king for a day,
just go to a mirror and look at yourself
and see what the face has to say.
For it isn't your father, mother or wife
whose judgment upon you must pass.
The person whose verdict
counts most in your life
is the one staring back from the glass.
You may fool the whole world
down the pathway of years
and get pats on the back as you pass.
But your final reward
will be heartache and tears
if you've cheated the face in the glass.

Habit #37

Admit When You are Wrong

I don't know of anyone who likes being wrong. What you've got to understand is most people have more respect for a person who admits they are wrong than a person who won't. You will be amazed how people will be more forgiving of a person who admits they are wrong. It takes courage to admit you made a mistake. It is also a true sign of maturity by owning up to your errors and then moving on. Not being able to admit you are wrong shows a lack of self-confidence. We are all going to misjudge, jump to wrong conclusions, assume, misread, guess, suppose, speculate, misinterpret, over-estimate, underestimate, and miscalculate; it's just human nature. People who have always got to be right or are inflexible and arrogant are unpleasant to be around. You don't want to associate, socialize or work with them; so don't be one. Admit you are wrong, learn from your error, and move on.

Habit #38
Listen Every Chance You Get

The need to listen to others is critical. Life is too short to be able to learn how to be successful all by yourself. If you want to profoundly increase your learning curve, start listening considerably more than you speak. You can't learn anything by being the person who is doing all the talking. We all have one tongue and two ears, which is a good way to remind ourselves that we should listen twice as much as we speak. You will be amazed at what you can learn from others if you just start listening. So start asking good questions, then close your mouth, listen, and learn.

Habit #39
Prepare a "Things To Do" List

You can either run your day or your day can run you. The key to being successful is for you to be the one running your day. Life is full of uncertainties and surprises that seem to come at you when you least expect them. Don't let them stop you from reaching your objective. Once you have established your goals, you must then start developing your plan of attack, what you need to do to achieve those goals. The perfect way to do that is to prepare a "Things To Do" list each night. You must prioritize the list in order of importance, with the most important on top. (A – items that must be done. B – items that need to be done, etc.) If you have multiple A's, then have A-1, A-2, A-3, and so on. Consult that list at least three times per day so it will help you keep on track, and then knock them out in order of priority. If you want to succeed, then strive to get your A's done every day. A *"Things To Do"* list will keep you on track; start one today.

Habit #40
Don't React - Get the Facts and Then Act

There are two sides to every story, and the key to a successful career or relationship is to hear both sides before determining how you should act. Jumping to conclusions or reacting prematurely before you have all the facts can sometimes lead to horrible consequences for one or both parties. Every day I receive e-mails from friends and clients containing some amazing stories. The problem is many of them aren't true. They sound true and contain some elements of fact, but the majority of the story is embellished or totally fabricated. By passing the story on to someone else before you validate its truthfulness, you are helping to perpetuate a false story which could prove to be extremely hurtful to the people in the story. The simple thing to do is never share rumors, stories, or e-mails with anyone until you personally have checked things out. If you can't prove it, don't share it.

Habit #41
Beware of Quick Fixes

Why is it we rarely have time to do it right the first time, but we always find time to do it right the second time? Anything worth doing is worth doing right the first time. Problems solved by quick fixes seldom stay fixed; therefore, it wasn't a fix, it was just a temporary remedy to a problem that still exists. Put to memory the 5-P formula – *Proper Planning Prevents Poor Performance.* It's great to be known as the person who can get things done fast, just as long as they are done right. Having to do something a second time is a total waste of time, money, and resources. Don't confuse this with failing to accomplish something you have never done before; those are learning experiences. What we are addressing is failing to achieve something for the mere reason of not reviewing, planning, and preparing properly before attempting the task. If it is worth fixing, it's worth fixing right the first time.

Habit #42
Become Courageous

The following is repeated by the cadets during chapel services at the U.S. Military Academy at West Point. I think it will help you in dealing with all the challenges, obstacles, vices, distractions, disputes, temptations, trials, and tribulations you will encounter in your lifetime. It takes a person of courage to overcome them and become successful.

Make us choose the harder right
instead of the easier wrong,
and never to be content with a half truth
when the whole truth can be won.
Endow us with the courage that is born of loyalty
to all that is noble and worthy,
that scorns to compromise
with vice and injustice and knows no fear
when truth and right
are in jeopardy.

Habit #43

Sometimes You Must Lose a Fight to Win a War

Always remember, if you are trying to win an argument, then you are also trying to make the other person lose that same argument. Your victory has also caused a defeat. When you defeat someone, you haven't endeared yourself to that person. On the contrary, many times you have alienated yourself from that individual. Everyone is entitled to their point of view. Sometimes by simply allowing a person to feel as if they are right, you can still get what you want. Words like "I can see your point" don't put the other person on the defensive. On the contrary, it shows you are willing to consider other possibilities, remedies, or solutions. Your objective should not be to win but to influence, help, inform, and enlighten. If you win, someone else lost, and no one likes losing. Always remember, **a person convinced against their will is a person still not convinced.**

Habit #44
Strive to Follow the Golden Rule

CHRISTIANITY:

*Do unto others as
you would have others do unto you.*

CONFUCIANISM:

*Do not unto others what
you would not have them do unto you.*

JUDAISM:

*Whatever is hurtful to yourself
do not to your fellow man.*

The Golden Rule is a
universally accepted principal.
You can never go wrong
incorporating it into your daily life.

Habit #45
Ask for Help and Advice

No one has enough time on earth to be able to learn it all. No one has enough time to read, research, experiment, and acquire everything you need to know to be successful. You need to take advantage of those who have come before you and learn from their experiences. It is easier to have someone explain to you how to do something rather than you stumbling around trying to figure it out on your own.

Smart people
learn from their mistakes.

Wise people
learn from other people's mistakes.

You can shorten your learning curve by simply asking those who *have been there and done it before* to share some of their wisdom. Successful people understand the importance of learning from others.

Habit #46
You Have to Stretch Yourself

It is amazing what you can accomplish when you put in the time, effort, and practice. In order to keep progressing, you have to keep pushing yourself, stretching to achieve more. Mavis Lingren, when she was 62 years old, decided she wanted to run a marathon. The day she decided her goal she couldn't run further than a block. Eight years later she ran her first marathon. At the age of 86, she ran in the New York City Marathon, her 65th marathon in 16 years. Roger Banister was the first person to run the mile in less than four minutes. The experts said it was physically impossible for a human to run a mile in less than four minutes. Roger Banister proved the experts wrong. The following year, after Banister proved it could be done, six other runners ran the mile in under four minutes. Every record is meant to be broken by those who are willing to stretch themselves. Your success is just a stretch away.

Habit #47
Act Like You Have Been There

When you score the winning touchdown, make the final shot at the buzzer, get the huge sales contract, get selected as the top employee for the year, or win whatever it is you really wanted to win, act like you have been there before. Be gracious in your winning moment because there will come a time when you don't win. By accomplishing the amazing feat and not making a big deal out of it, you will cause even more of a stir in the minds of others. Folks will be wondering how good you are when you don't make a big deal out of something. It is better for others to say how good you are than for you to say it or try to show it. Carry yourself with confidence, show excitement for your feat, but always act like you've been there. Jack Nicklaus raised his putter and nodded to the crowd after making an incredible shot; he didn't pound his chest in a display of egotism of how great he was. Be gracious in winning, humble in defeat, and always confident.

Habit #48
Handle Jerks Quickly and Cautiously

"Jerks" are difficult people to deal with because they don't care about reasoning, and they especially don't care about you. Screaming, yelling, ranting, or raving at them won't help either because they are not listening. Those tactics only serve to worsen matters. To end a situation with a "Jerk," you must first understand that you are not dealing with a rational person. Reasoning with them in any way will not work, so you need to minimize your losses. Deal with a "Jerk" the same way you deal with stepping in manure; clean off your shoe, remember the displeasure in cleaning your shoe, and then remember where you stepped, so you won't step there again. You must have the frame of mind that you didn't lose, because you were dealing with a "Jerk." In simpler terms: *Hold your tongue, and move on.*

Habit #49
You Have Got to Take the Shot

It is a simple rule: *You can't make the shot until you take the shot.* Many a career failed because someone was just too scared to take the shot. Michael Jordan, probably the best pro basketball player to ever play the game, missed 50 percent of the game winning shots he took. The key is, he took the shot. More importantly, he wanted to be the one who took the last shot. He wasn't concerned or thinking about the consequences of missing the shot. Success does not come to the timid or meek. In fact, **success does not come to anyone; you must go out and get it.** If you don't ask, you won't get. If you don't try, you have already failed. Prepare yourself; practice, drill and rehearse, then let it rip. If it doesn't work, then rethink, reload, and take another shot. *The only difference in a big shot from a little shot is the big shot was a little shot who just kept on shooting.*

Habit #50
Treat Everyone Special

On your journey to being successful, you will encounter all types of people. You will meet folks who are talented, motivated, rich, and/or powerful. You will also encounter folks who are less fortunate; people who, due to no fault of their own, haven't achieved any status, privilege, money, or recognition in life. It doesn't matter who they are or what their status is, you must treat them all the same by treating them "special." People love to feel important, exceptional, extraordinary, or elite. By taking a few extra moments to be genuinely interested in others, you will greatly enhance your personal potential for success. You will never know when they might return your polite attitude or act of kindness with something which may prove to be extremely beneficial to you. Just make it a habit, regardless of their status, to treat everyone special.

Habit # 51
Protect Your Integrity

Everything in life can be taken away from you: your money, your home, your car, and all your worldly possessions. You can lose your good health or even your life. The only thing that cannot be taken away is your integrity. Only you can give it up by lying, cheating, and/or stealing. Integrity is a quality a person gives to themselves, so guard it, protect it, value it, and respect it. Once you give up your integrity, you can seldom, if ever, get it back. I once read that when you base your life on sound moral principles, ninety-nine percent of your decisions are already made. When you live a life based on integrity, you will never have anything to fear because you will have nothing to hide.

Habit #52
Don't Procrastinate - It Kills Dreams

You need to deal with whatever is holding you back. Many people create excuses or blame others for their inability to do what is necessary to become successful. The only thing really holding you back from reaching your desired goals is you. I think Benjamin Franklin summed it up quite well when he said, *"Never leave till tomorrow that which you can do today."* Remove the clutter in your life and focus on where it is you want to go, and then do it. Seek out slivers of time everywhere you can *(go to bed late, wake up early, take a shorter lunch, turn off the TV)* to use towards accomplishing your goals. As the Nike slogan says, *"Just Do It."* You have everything to gain and nothing to lose because you now know there is no such thing as failure, only learning experiences disguised as temporary setbacks. Keep saying it every day …

If it is to be, it's up to ME!

Conclusion

Your Choices Will Determine Your Success

Choose to   live a life of excellence

Choose to   rise above trivial things

Choose to   be courageous

Choose to   control your destiny

Choose to   never give up

Choose to   guard your integrity

Choose to   be punctual, orderly, and diligent

Choose to   believe in yourself

Choose to   live a life of action, not words

Choose to   practice, drill, and rehearse

Choose to   be a positive person

Choose to   never quit learning

Choose to   make the 52 habits a part of your daily life

And by making these choices,
you have now chosen to be successful.

Epilogue

An unknown author once wrote a list of simple rules that when combined with my 52 habits will also help to improve your chance for success.

If you open it, close it.
If you turn it on, turn it off.
If you unlock it, lock it up.
If you break it, admit it.
If you can't fix it, call someone who can.
If you borrow it, return it.
If you value it, take care of it.
If you move it, put it back.
If it belongs to someone else, get permission to use it.
If you don't know how to operate it, leave it alone.
If it's none of your business, don't ask questions.

Now, go out there and

Make The 52 Work for You.

As I promised in my introduction,
here are your copies of the
52 Essential Habits For Success.

May I suggest
you go back over them often,
just to refresh and sharpen
your memory.

Habit #1
Believe in Yourself

If you don't believe in yourself, why should anyone else believe in you? Sure you are going to make mistakes; that is part of life. People want to be around confident people. One of the most important traits of any leader is their confidence in themselves. People don't want to follow someone who lacks self-confidence. When you first start out, you may have to *fake it before you make it;* that is okay. All of us at one time in our lives were young and inexperienced. None of us were born with all the knowledge, experience and talents we would need to be successful. These are all developed skills. So relax and learn from your mistakes, realizing we have all passed this way before. Have the confidence to tell yourself you will get it, learn it, or figure it out. It might take you a while, but realize you know you have what it takes to do it. Start believing in yourself, and others will start believing in you, too.

Habit #2
Act as if the World is Watching

Thomas Jefferson said, "*Whenever you are to do a thing, though it can never be known but to yourself, ask yourself how you would act were the world looking at you, and act accordingly.*" Even though that was said over 200 years ago, it is still great advice for today, especially in this technological world with people carrying mini video-recorders in their cell phones. The next thing you know, your actions are being shown on national TV or on the Internet for all the world to see. So act as if there is a camera on you at all times and act accordingly. The great philosopher Seneca said,

> "*I will govern my life and thoughts as if the whole world were to see the one and to read the other.*"

Habit #3
Practice, Drill & Rehearse,
Then Take the Initiative

If you want to beat your competition, then you have to be willing to put in the time to *practice, drill, and rehearse* (PDR). The great ones don't need someone telling them to practice. They understand when they are not practicing, someone else is, and when they meet that person on the field of competition, that person will win. Success comes to those who take the initiative to do more, stay longer, and work harder. The day you understand your success is dependent on you - *your own desire, initiative, and fortitude* - is the day you start achieving greatness. To the great ones, PDR is not a motto on some wall, it is a way of life. Simply stated:

If you want to be the best at what you do, then practice more than the rest, and success will come to you.

Habit #4
Don't be Afraid to Fail

It's amazing how much experience can be gained by making a mistake. As Henry Ford once stated: *"Failure is the opportunity to begin again more intelligently."* If you never try to do something beyond what you already know how to do, you will never get any better. Failure is a major component to your success process. You didn't learn to walk after your first try, or feed yourself, talk, ride a bike, or play a musical instrument. There were a multitude of attempts before you became proficient at any of these. Notice, I said attempts, not failures. You need to decide that *there are no failures in life, only results.* Failure isn't fatal unless you quit. If you didn't like the results, then analyze what went wrong, learn, and then alter your method. The failed attempt will merely teach you that your method was flawed; so correct it and try again. Failure is something that happens to you; it's an event, not a person.

Habit #5
Make Goal Setting a Habit

If you don't know where you are going, then how will you know when you get there? The vast majority of people don't set goals, and the vast majority of people do not reach their full potential, thus limiting their level of success. I think you will find a correlation there. You have got to decide what it is you want and **write it down;** some call it "thinking on paper". You then have to decide what it is you will have to do to make what you have written down become a reality. The first two steps in making a dream become a reality are to write it down and then set a deadline. Remember to be "SMART" about your goals: *Specific, Measurable, Attainable, Realistic, and Timely.* Determining your goals will determine your actions which, when accomplished, will determine your success. It has been proven that people with goals earn twice as much as those without goals. Being successful starts with establishing your goals.

Habit #6
You Must Pay the Price

One of the most valuable things you possess is your willpower. Great accomplishments come from great efforts. You will have to pay a price if you are to be successful. Hard work, practice, patience, sacrifice, and rehearsing are all words **Super Achievers** understand. The question is: are you willing to **Pay the Price** for greatness? What you say, what you wish for, and what you hope for doesn't count. Your actions are all that matter. Your actions are the only thing that will get you success. The price of mediocrity is far less than the price of greatness. It is easier to settle for being average than to strive for greatness. The choice is yours and yours alone.

Habit #7
Never, Never, Never Give Up

Elbert Hubbard captures the point I am trying to make so profoundly in his words: *"There is no defeat except in no longer trying. There is no defeat save within …"* Failure is just a result in the learning process; giving up is a choice. Walt Disney was fired for lack of creativity and went bankrupt twice before he was able to turn his dream into a reality. At one time Donald Trump had a negative net worth of $900 million. Most people would have declared bankruptcy. Seven years later he was worth over $2 billion. It took Ray Kroc, founder of McDonald's, twenty-seven years to make his first million. Bill Gates' first Microsoft company went bankrupt. He then became the richest man in the world. Giving up is a choice, a very bad choice.

Habit # 8
Hang Out with Successful People

If you want to be successful, then you need to "hang out" with successful people. Watch what they do and how they work at their chosen profession. Unconsciously, you will start adapting these behaviors, habits, attitudes, and opinions of these successful individuals. Dr. David McClelland of Harvard found, after twenty-five years of research, that the choice of a "negative reference group" is enough to condemn a person to failure and underachievement in life. The good doctor simply means, ***if you hang out with people who are going nowhere with their lives, then you'll be headed in that same direction.*** If you can't be around successful people, then read as many biographies/autobiographies as you can about successful people. Personally, I would rather be by myself than with people who are headed nowhere. What will you choose?

Habit # 9
Success Requires Self-Discipline

Self-discipline is making yourself do what you need to do when you need to do it whether you want to or not. In the overall scheme of success, being self-disciplined is the most important trait you must possess. You can know, understand, and identify what must be done, but if you don't have the discipline to do it, it's all for naught. The true test of your character lies in your self-discipline. Your persistence to make things happen, your resolve, and your willpower will determine just how successful you will be in life. There will be days you won't feel like getting up and doing what needs to be done. Those are the days your character is being tested. The great ones get it done regardless of how they feel. Remember your action statement:

If it is to be, it's up to me.

Habit #10
Accept Criticism
for the Benefits it Brings

There is nothing fun about receiving criticism. It is amazing how painful words can be if we let them. It was once said: **"There is nothing either good or bad but thinking makes it so."** So channel the criticizing words differently. Regardless of the agenda of the person giving the criticism, use the words to your betterment even if they were given for someone else's gain. This is all about creating a better you, not a better them. Filter out all pain and prejudice and allow only the things that will benefit you to enter your mind. Dr. Norman Vincent Peale stated: *"The trouble with most of us is that we would rather be ruined with praise than saved with criticism."* Sometimes the only way you are going to know if you are doing something wrong is by someone telling you. Criticism is therefore helpful and should be accepted in that manner.

Habit #11
Contain Your Anger

Anger is a self–induced reaction to an external stimulus. In other words, something happened that you didn't like, and you got angry. Outbursts of anger can cause stress, heart attacks, ulcers, headaches, lack of control, saying things we don't mean, fights, and retaliations, all of which are bad. The amazing thing about anger is that it is unnecessary. Anger comes from within you. It is a response you choose to give when you feel you are being victimized, treated unfairly, cheated, or taken advantage of. The next time you feel your anger raising up its ugly head, take a moment and get control, making certain that you don't say a word. Remember, the person screaming in an argument is the person losing the argument. You can respond in an angry manner or a calm one. Anger is a choice, not a cause or condition.

Habit #12
Smile - It's Good for You and Those Around You

There are thousands of languages we don't understand, but yet a smile is understood no matter what language is being spoken. To successfully deal with people, you need to create trust, confidence, and rapport. It is a proven fact that the simple physical response of a smile will help to create all three. If you want to be more successful, have less stress, more friends, and better health, then smile more. Smiling is good for you, and it's good for the people around you. Make it a habit to smile when you are greeting anyone. When you are asking someone for help, smile. If you want to change your negative state of mind, smile. People want to be around people who are in good moods, and being in a good mood all starts with a smile. Smiling displays your frame of mind and warmth without having to say a word, and it puts you in a positive mood; this is all good.

Habit #13
Look for Ways to Praise Often

If you want to have a lot of friends in business and in your personal life, then look for ways to compliment *(praise)* them often. Make sure it is sincere praise and not contrived. Think how great you feel when someone tells you that you did a good job. Complimenting someone is not a hard thing to do, but we seem to forget to do it, even when the perfect opportunity avails itself. If you make it a habit to praise people rather than condemn, you will be amazed how many people will want to help you. Making people feel good about themselves will never do you any harm. On the contrary, it will do nothing but good for you. There is an old saying that will benefit you greatly if you utilize it. *You can get whatever you want if you help other people get what they want.* Go out of your way to compliment people, and your journey to success will become easier.

Habit #14
Shorten Your Learning Curve
by Reading

Life is too short for you to learn all there is to know by personal experience. Reading is an excellent way to shorten your learning curve. The gifts of knowledge, insight, wisdom, and experience can all be bestowed upon you if you will merely take the time to read what brilliant people have written. The great self-help and inspirational author Og Mandino once wrote, *"the only difference in you now and you five years from now, are the people you meet and the things that you read."* I would take heed to his words. Reading will improve your creativity, vocabulary, spelling, and language skills. Make it a part of your daily routine to read something (*at least five days per week*) that will help you become a better person, spouse, friend, associate, parent, athlete, student, employee, and/or boss. Becoming a smarter person is only a book away.

Habit #15
Never Neglect Your Body

When you neglect your body, your energy levels diminish, fatigue sets in, and illness ensues. Exercise is a key factor in all aspects of your success. There is a litany of incredible benefits to your overall health if you maintain a proper exercise program. Physical activity reduces stress, increases energy, gives you greater stamina, helps manage your weight, improves muscle tone, aids in digestion, helps you relax, clears your mind, gives you a better outlook on life (more positive and optimistic), enhances your sexual response, increases alertness, improves sleep, and may possibly reduce your need for certain medications. So get up and get moving with some kind of structured exercise program a minimum of three times per week. Remember, ***if you don't use it, you will lose it.***

Habit #16
Be Positive
It's the Only Way to Act

Being negative causes stress, illness, worry, anger, reduces productivity, takes the fun out of life, and makes others not want to be around you. You are going to have bad days, equipment failures, traffic congestion, delays, spills, mistakes, misunderstandings, dealings with jerks and idiots, car problems, and unexpected expenses (to name just a few) in your life. The remarkable thing about life is every moment we have a choice regarding the attitude we embrace. If I have the choice, I would rather be around a positive person than a negative one. Olympic gold medalist figure skater Scott Hamilton stated, ***"the only disability in life is a bad attitude."*** It doesn't mean bad things don't happen to positive people. It just means positive people don't let bad things hold them back. Having a positive attitude doesn't guarantee your success, but it's a great place to start.

Habit #17
Watch What You Say

Remember what Jefferson said in Habit #2, *"… act were the world looking at you, and act accordingly."* Things have a way of coming back to haunt you. People take things out of context to support their own personal agenda. I think the best rule to follow is to say nothing about anyone you wouldn't have the courage to say directly to their face. Stick to what you know to be factual, not on hearsay or rumor. Someday you may have to defend your comments, so make sure you speak only the truth. Most of the problems you will encounter in your life are people problems. Most of those problems stem from what someone said or did. So select your words wisely, positively, and according to facts, because having to eat them later is not a pleasurable experience.

Habit #18
Want an Advantage – Be Early

If you want to reduce your stress, then be early. If you want to impress your boss, coach, or teacher, then be early. Being late shows a lack of respect for whomever you're dealing with. I'm not talking about going to a party and being the first one there. We'll have to deal with the proper social etiquette at another time. I am talking about virtually everything else. Staying ahead of the game, ahead of the deadline, ahead of when you have to be somewhere, and ahead of when the project is due will forever endear you to those who are expecting anything on time. Being early shows others you are motivated, organized, and disciplined. Be known as the one they can always count on to be early, prepared, and excited to be there, and you will have everyone wanting you on their team. True leaders don't keep people waiting.

Habit #19
Do More Than Expected

If you want to position yourself for success, then always do more than expected. By incorporating this one single habit into everything you do, you will basically be guaranteeing your success in life. The people who do the minimum required will usually get the minimum return. All great athletes, musicians, actors, lawyers, doctors, business people, etc., etc., understand for them to excel at their profession, they have to be willing to do more than those around them. You will never become an exceptional athlete by practicing the bare minimum. The great ones are forever practicing, working out, and studying their sport more than their competition. Whatever the task, do more than expected, and I can assure you your life will turn out better than you expected.

Habit #20
Say "Thank You" Often

Two of the most powerful words in the English language are *"thank you."* These two words are so simple to say, but so seldom used. You can carry it even further with words such as: *"I really appreciate that." "You were so kind to help me." "I couldn't have done this without you." "You were such a big help to me."* We get so caught up in the speed of our daily lives that we forget to say the words that will help make people want to assist us again. Regardless of your position or status in life, you should never forget to say these two words. When someone lets you cut in a line of traffic and they can't hear the words, you can still mouth them so they see that you are saying "thank you." Some people would simply call this common courtesy; I call it required courtesy for a successful life.

Habit #21
Remember People's Names

The words that are most familiar to you and the least threatening are the words that make up your name. If you want to get someone to relax, make yourself seem more acceptable to them, present yourself as less intimidating, then start or finish your opening statement to them by incorporating their name into the sentence. When you first meet someone, try saying their name several times while you are speaking to them so it will help you better remember their name when they leave. People will be extremely impressed if you have just met them and you remember their name the next time you see them. It is a sure way of showing your respect to them by proving their name was important enough for you to remember it.

Habit #22
Let Them Know You Care

There is enormous power in sending cards, notes, or letters to people. Using the Internet to stay in touch with friends, associates, and clients is helpful, but if you want to stand out from the rest of the crowd, send them something they don't have to print off on their printer. If you want to really stand out, remember people on special occasions, holidays, and especially their birthday. Former President George H.W. Bush used to spend two hours every night writing notes to friends, family, and acquaintances. People will appreciate the fact that you went to the trouble to not only remember them, but also took the time to handwrite a simple message. Putting that message in a nice card would be even better. Always remember, **people don't care how much you know until they know how much you care.**

Habit #23
Always Use Good Manners

In this fast-paced techno-gadget world where people text rather than talk, e-mail rather than converse, and hurry rather than help, **a person who shows a little common courtesy will be the exception rather than the norm.** Opening doors for folks, pulling out chairs, letting someone else go first, waiting for everyone to be served before you start eating are all just simple, courteous gestures, but they say volumes about the type of person you are. These gestures are not just for the special people; they are for everyone. I don't like to be around people who are rude, arrogant, loud, and obnoxious or who don't have the decency to treat everyone with proper respect, regardless of their socioeconomic status. Treat everyone as if they were your equal, and always **shower them with courtesy and good manners.**

Habit #24
Beware of Fads

Fads come and go. The problem with that statement is that they go. The desire to stay up with the latest fashion trends, wear the "right" clothes or tattoo, drive the "hot" car, have the latest cell phone or technological gadget isn't new. It was that way 50 years ago, and it will be the same 50 years from now. I am not going to address what makes people "cool." My concern comes when a fad has something to do with permanently altering your body. The tattoo you love today, you may hate ten years from now. When it comes to doing permanent things to your body such as tattoos, piercing, and brands, I would suggest you give it serious thought and never do it on a whim or a dare. Permanent is a big commitment to something that may not be "cool" later on in your life. You can buy new cars and clothes and get rid of the old ones, but permanent is forever.

Habit #25

Pay Attention to Your First Impression

You will never get a second chance to make a good first impression, so that first impression really matters. You want the way you look to demand respect. People like to deal with individuals who are successful, and that means you need to look the part. I always feel if a person doesn't respect their own appearance, then what other things do they have little respect for? It doesn't take a huge income to be clean and well-groomed with clothes pressed and shoes polished. I will be grading you the moment you walk in the door, so get my attention by paying attention to yourself. Companies don't want an unkempt, disheveled, messy, uncombed person representing them. A critical part of being professional is looking professional. If you want someone to pay attention to you, then you must first pay attention to yourself.

Habit #26

Prepare Now or Fail Later

The great college basketball coach John Wooden (who won 88 consecutive games, 11 NCAA national championships, 7 of them in a row) had a saying: ***"Failure to prepare is preparing to fail."*** The truly successful people leave nothing to chance. They put in the time, effort, research, and thought to ensure they will achieve their desired goal. You don't climb Mount Everest by showing up with some climbing gear and start to climb. You spend months planning out the entire journey, day by day, moment by moment. This is your life and you've got one shot at it. All success begins with a definite purpose, a specific objective, and a plan to achieve it. It's your choice; ***prepare now or fail later.***

Habit #27

Show Excitement in Your Greetings

I have never seen a dog, when its master walks in the door, turn its head and say *"Yo! I had a bad day. Not enough water, not enough dog food, you didn't leave the air conditioner on 72°, and the cat has got to go."* A dog is always happy to see its master. The tail is wagging; it's jumping around acting like it hasn't seen its master in months. A dog doesn't do it some of the time; it does it all the time. What a great feeling the dog gives to its master. The simple expression of *I am really happy to see you* makes anyone feel good. I am not telling you to jump around and look foolish every time you see someone. But I am suggesting you get up, make eye contact, give them a smile, and show a genuine interest in them. You will find that people will love to be around you, look forward to seeing you, and include you in their plans, parties, and get-togethers. People love dogs because dogs love people, and they show it. The key words are, "they show it" **every time**.

Habit #28
Be Persistent, Relentless, Determined

What will separate you from those average souls out there who stay mired in mediocrity will be your willpower, your desire to see it through, to not fail, to pay the price to achieve success. Always think your next great victory is just about to happen. Thomas Edison failed over 11,000 times trying to invent the light bulb. A person one time asked him what it felt like failing over 11,000 times. Mr. Edison said, *"I didn't fail 11,000 times. I discovered 11,000 ways how not to do it."* Some of the greatest success stories ever written are about people who overcame incredible adversities, obstacles, and/or rejections. They just kept working at it, refining their skills, or changing their methods until they made it. The difference between average and great starts with relentlessly applying all your physical and mental talents **to one task at a time** until you have completed the task.

Habit #29
Search Out Role Models

In most cases, you aren't the first person to ever attempt your chosen goal. If you want to be great at your chosen profession, remember, others have passed this way before you who have learned great lessons they would love to share. You might not be able to talk to Michael Jordan one on one, but you can read about his life and how he became an incredible basketball player. In many cases, there are people who would love to share the lessons they have learned if you just ask them. People love a compliment. Approaching someone and asking for their help because you respect what they have accomplished and would like to learn from them is a great compliment to them. Remember, to receive help you have to ask for help.

Habit #30
Never Waste Time

When you are wasting your time, you are wasting your life. Your life is a finite amount of time made up of moments. Each moment, second, minute, hour, day that passes can never be relived or re-captured. Why would you waste a limited resource, an irreplaceable commodity that you can never get back? Successful people take full advantage of their time. They plan their day ahead of time. Time management skills are an essential tool for anyone who wants to be successful. You can do nothing about the time you have already lost, but you can do everything with the time you have left. **Every minute spent in planning your day saves about ten minutes in executing it.** If you are to accomplish your goals, then you will need to be productive and efficient with your time management. If you are not planning your day, then your day will be planning you.

Habit #31
Always Be Truthful

The truth is but a simple thing, for it knows no right or
wrong. There are those who would alter it
to make the truth be gone.

They will speak, imply, suggest what you know are not
the facts. But the truth will remain the same,
rest assured it will be back.

It may be for the moment, the truth is not revealed.
There you stand betrayed by one,
accused of what's not real.

But for those of us who have been wronged,
take solace in what I say.
There will come a time where all will know
in some uncertain way.

The truth will rise above it all and prove their words
were wrong, causing those who spoke the words,
reputations now be gone.

The truth is but a simple thing, it may be hard to say.
The truth is but a simple thing,
and for me the only way.

Habit #32
Don't Gossip – It's a Waste of Time

What do you accomplish when you gossip about other people? Nothing, except wasting time. You haven't learned a thing, you have helped no one, and you have accomplished nothing. I hate to use such a simple adage, but I can think of no other way to say it better. **If you can't say something nice about someone, then don't say it.** Don't get yourself caught up in the bashing, trashing, smashing, gossiping conversations. By wasting your precious time in this common activity, you are really hurting yourself. Why would you ever want to do that? We have already established the importance of not wasting time, and gossiping is a huge time waster. *Always ask yourself … is what I am doing now taking me closer to where it is I want to go?* If the answer is no, then stop what you are doing and get back on track.

Habit #33

Concentrate on
Your Strengths & Interests

When you focus most of your time and energy on things you are good at, you will reap enormous rewards. Sometimes your strengths will be hidden in your interests. Don't try to be something your physical or mental abilities won't allow you to be. Focus on what you can do rather than on things you can't. If you aren't certain where your strengths lie, then focus on things you enjoy doing rather than on things you hate. Couple your interests with your strengths, and then commit to concentrated practice and study. Your concerted efforts will reap you enormous rewards, and you will also enjoy your journey towards success.

Habit #34
Become Interested in Others

Shakespeare wrote, *"The fragrance of a rose lingers on the hand that casts it."* Bestowing positive sentiments on or about others will eventually find a way back to you. Talk to people about what interests them, not you, and listen attentively. Getting people to talk about their favorite subject (themselves) is easy. Just start asking questions. To paraphrase Kipling, *"six honest serving men taught me all I knew; their names were What, Why, When, How, Where and Who."* Your objective in any conversation is to be listening more than you are speaking. Try and resist complaining about or criticizing others. By showing appreciation and admiration, by being agreeable and accepting, you will be a welcomed participant in any conversation. Being interested in others makes them more interested in you.

Habit #35
Expand Your Vocabulary

There are over 650,000 words in the English language. The average person knows about 15,000 and a child of 5 knows about 5,000. A very scary statistic is that after the age of 30, the average person learns about 5 words per year. If we live to be 75 years old, this would mean a person currently 30 years of age will learn an additional 225 words the rest of their life. If you want to set yourself apart from the masses, start with learning one new word per week. That would mean a 30-year-old person would learn an additional 2,340 words over the rest of their life rather than a paltry 225. The use of an excellent vocabulary will distinguish you from others and is usually an excellent indicator you are an intelligent person. So if you want to appear smart, then work on expanding your vocabulary.

Habit #36
Don't Cheat the Face in the Glass

Below is a poem by an unknown author I have taken the liberty to paraphrase. I feel it best addresses **Cheating Yourself.**

When you get what you want
in your struggle for self
and the world makes you king for a day,
just go to a mirror and look at yourself
and see what the face has to say.
For it isn't your father, mother or wife
whose judgment upon you must pass.
The person whose verdict
counts most in your life
is the one staring back from the glass.
You may fool the whole world
down the pathway of years
and get pats on the back as you pass.
But your final reward
will be heartache and tears
if you've cheated the face in the glass.

Habit #37
Admit When You are Wrong

I don't know of anyone who likes being wrong. What you've got to understand is most people have more respect for a person who admits they are wrong than a person who won't. You will be amazed how people will be more forgiving of a person who admits they are wrong. It takes courage to admit you made a mistake. It is also a true sign of maturity by owning up to your errors and then moving on. Not being able to admit you are wrong shows a lack of self-confidence. We are all going to misjudge, jump to wrong conclusions, assume, misread, guess, suppose, speculate, misinterpret, over-estimate, underestimate, and miscalculate; it's just human nature. People who have always got to be right or are inflexible and arrogant are unpleasant to be around. You don't want to associate, socialize or work with them; so don't be one. Admit you are wrong, learn from your error, and move on.

Habit #38
Listen Every Chance You Get

The need to listen to others is critical. Life is too short to be able to learn how to be successful all by yourself. If you want to profoundly increase your learning curve, start listening considerably more than you speak. You can't learn anything by being the person who is doing all the talking. We all have one tongue and two ears, which is a good way to remind ourselves that we should listen twice as much as we speak. You will be amazed at what you can learn from others if you just start listening. So start asking good questions, then close your mouth, listen, and learn.

Habit #39
Prepare a "Things To Do" List

You can either run your day or your day can run you. The key to being successful is for you to be the one running your day. Life is full of uncertainties and surprises that seem to come at you when you least expect them. Don't let them stop you from reaching your objective. Once you have established your goals, you must then start developing your plan of attack, what you need to do to achieve those goals. The perfect way to do that is to prepare a "Things To Do" list each night. You must prioritize the list in order of importance, with the most important on top. (A – items that must be done. B – items that need to be done, etc.) If you have multiple A's, then have A-1, A-2, A-3, and so on. Consult that list at least three times per day so it will help you keep on track, and then knock them out in order of priority. If you want to succeed, then strive to get your A's done every day. A ***"Things To Do"*** list will keep you on track; start one today.

Habit #40
Don't React - Get the Facts and Then Act

There are two sides to every story, and the key to a successful career or relationship is to hear both sides before determining how you should act. Jumping to conclusions or reacting prematurely before you have all the facts can sometimes lead to horrible consequences for one or both parties. Every day I receive e-mails from friends and clients containing some amazing stories. The problem is many of them aren't true. They sound true and contain some elements of fact, but the majority of the story is embellished or totally fabricated. By passing the story on to someone else before you validate its truthfulness, you are helping to perpetuate a false story which could prove to be extremely hurtful to the people in the story. The simple thing to do is never share rumors, stories, or e-mails with anyone until you personally have checked things out. If you can't prove it, don't share it.

Habit #41
Beware of Quick Fixes

Why is it we rarely have time to do it right the first time, but we always find time to do it right the second time? Anything worth doing is worth doing right the first time. Problems solved by quick fixes seldom stay fixed; therefore, it wasn't a fix, it was just a temporary remedy to a problem that still exists. Put to memory the 5-P formula – *Proper Planning Prevents Poor Performance.* It's great to be known as the person who can get things done fast, just as long as they are done right. Having to do something a second time is a total waste of time, money, and resources. Don't confuse this with failing to accomplish something you have never done before; those are learning experiences. What we are addressing is failing to achieve something for the mere reason of not reviewing, planning, and preparing properly before attempting the task. If it is worth fixing, it's worth fixing right the first time.

Habit #42
Become Courageous

The following is repeated by the cadets during chapel services at the U.S. Military Academy at West Point. I think it will help you in dealing with all the challenges, obstacles, vices, distractions, disputes, temptations, trials, and tribulations you will encounter in your lifetime. It takes a person of courage to overcome them and become successful.

Make us choose the harder right
instead of the easier wrong,
and never to be content with a half truth
when the whole truth can be won.
Endow us with the courage that is born of loyalty
to all that is noble and worthy,
that scorns to compromise
with vice and injustice and knows no fear
when truth and right
are in jeopardy.

Habit #43
Sometimes You Must Lose a Fight to Win a War

Always remember, if you are trying to win an argument, then you are also trying to make the other person lose that same argument. Your victory has also caused a defeat. When you defeat someone, you haven't endeared yourself to that person. On the contrary, many times you have alienated yourself from that individual. Everyone is entitled to their point of view. Sometimes by simply allowing a person to feel as if they are right, you can still get what you want. Words like "I can see your point" don't put the other person on the defensive. On the contrary, it shows you are willing to consider other possibilities, remedies, or solutions. Your objective should not be to win but to influence, help, inform, and enlighten. If you win, someone else lost, and no one likes losing. Always remember, **a person convinced against their will is a person still not convinced.**

Habit #44
Strive to Follow the Golden Rule

CHRISTIANITY:

*Do unto others as
you would have others do unto you.*

CONFUCIANISM:

*Do not unto others what
you would not have them do unto you.*

JUDAISM:

*Whatever is hurtful to yourself
do not to your fellow man.*

The Golden Rule is a
universally accepted principal.
You can never go wrong
incorporating it into your daily life.

Habit #45
Ask for Help and Advice

No one has enough time on earth to be able to learn it all. No one has enough time to read, research, experiment, and acquire everything you need to know to be successful. You need to take advantage of those who have come before you and learn from their experiences. It is easier to have someone explain to you how to do something rather than you stumbling around trying to figure it out on your own.

Smart people
learn from their mistakes.

Wise people
learn from other people's mistakes.

You can shorten your learning curve by simply asking those who *have been there and done it before* to share some of their wisdom. Successful people understand the importance of learning from others.

Habit #46
You Have to Stretch Yourself

It is amazing what you can accomplish when you put in the time, effort, and practice. In order to keep progressing, you have to keep pushing yourself, stretching to achieve more. Mavis Lingren, when she was 62 years old, decided she wanted to run a marathon. The day she decided her goal she couldn't run further than a block. Eight years later she ran her first marathon. At the age of 86, she ran in the New York City Marathon, her 65th marathon in 16 years. Roger Banister was the first person to run the mile in less than four minutes. The experts said it was physically impossible for a human to run a mile in less than four minutes. Roger Banister proved the experts wrong. The following year, after Banister proved it could be done, six other runners ran the mile in under four minutes. Every record is meant to be broken by those who are willing to stretch themselves. Your success is just a stretch away.

Habit #47
Act Like You Have Been There

When you score the winning touchdown, make the final shot at the buzzer, get the huge sales contract, get selected as the top employee for the year, or win whatever it is you really wanted to win, act like you have been there before. Be gracious in your winning moment because there will come a time when you don't win. By accomplishing the amazing feat and not making a big deal out of it, you will cause even more of a stir in the minds of others. Folks will be wondering how good you are when you don't make a big deal out of something. It is better for others to say how good you are than for you to say it or try to show it. Carry yourself with confidence, show excitement for your feat, but always act like you've been there. Jack Nicklaus raised his putter and nodded to the crowd after making an incredible shot; he didn't pound his chest in a display of egotism of how great he was. Be gracious in winning, humble in defeat, and always confident.

Habit #48

Handle Jerks Quickly and Cautiously

"Jerks" are difficult people to deal with because they don't care about reasoning, and they especially don't care about you. Screaming, yelling, ranting, or raving at them won't help either because they are not listening. Those tactics only serve to worsen matters. To end a situation with a "Jerk," you must first understand that you are not dealing with a rational person. Reasoning with them in any way will not work, so you need to minimize your losses. Deal with a "Jerk" the same way you deal with stepping in manure; clean off your shoe, remember the displeasure in cleaning your shoe, and then remember where you stepped, so you won't step there again. You must have the frame of mind that you didn't lose, because you were dealing with a "Jerk." In simpler terms: *Hold your tongue, and move on.*

Habit #49

You Have Got to Take the Shot

It is a simple rule: *You can't make the shot until you take the shot.* Many a career failed because someone was just too scared to take the shot. Michael Jordan, probably the best pro basketball player to ever play the game, missed 50 percent of the game winning shots he took. The key is, he took the shot. More importantly, he wanted to be the one who took the last shot. He wasn't concerned or thinking about the consequences of missing the shot. Success does not come to the timid or meek. In fact, **success does not come to anyone; you must go out and get it.** If you don't ask, you won't get. If you don't try, you have already failed. Prepare yourself; practice, drill and rehearse, then let it rip. If it doesn't work, then rethink, reload, and take another shot. *The only difference in a big shot from a little shot is the big shot was a little shot who just kept on shooting.*

Habit #50
Treat Everyone Special

On your journey to being successful, you will encounter all types of people. You will meet folks who are talented, motivated, rich, and/or powerful. You will also encounter folks who are less fortunate; people who, due to no fault of their own, haven't achieved any status, privilege, money, or recognition in life. It doesn't matter who they are or what their status is, you must treat them all the same by treating them "special." People love to feel important, exceptional, extraordinary, or elite. By taking a few extra moments to be genuinely interested in others, you will greatly enhance your personal potential for success. You will never know when they might return your polite attitude or act of kindness with something which may prove to be extremely beneficial to you. Just make it a habit, regardless of their status, to treat everyone special.

Habit # 51
Protect Your Integrity

Everything in life can be taken away from you: your money, your home, your car, and all your worldly possessions. You can lose your good health or even your life. The only thing that cannot be taken away is your integrity. Only you can give it up by lying, cheating, and/or stealing. Integrity is a quality a person gives to themselves, so guard it, protect it, value it, and respect it. Once you give up your integrity, you can seldom, if ever, get it back. I once read that when you base your life on sound moral principles, ninety-nine percent of your decisions are already made. When you live a life based on integrity, you will never have anything to fear because you will have nothing to hide.

Habit #52

Don't Procrastinate - It Kills Dreams

You need to deal with whatever is holding you back. Many people create excuses or blame others for their inability to do what is necessary to become successful. The only thing really holding you back from reaching your desired goals is you. I think Benjamin Franklin summed it up quite well when he said, *"Never leave till tomorrow that which you can do today."* Remove the clutter in your life and focus on where it is you want to go, and then do it. Seek out slivers of time everywhere you can *(go to bed late, wake up early, take a shorter lunch, turn off the TV)* to use towards accomplishing your goals. As the Nike slogan says, *"Just Do It."* You have everything to gain and nothing to lose because you now know there is no such thing as failure, only learning experiences disguised as temporary setbacks. Keep saying it every day …

If it is to be, it's up to ME!

How to Soar Like An Eagle
in a World Full of Turkeys

If you liked *52 Essential Habits For Success,* then it is a sure bet you will want to read Mr. Stevenson's first book, *How to Soar Like An Eagle in a World Full of Turkeys.* This best-selling book is a practical guide for both personal and professional achievement. The book is full of winning strategies, techniques, methods, thoughts, and key principles for a well-balanced life that will empower you towards a better future.

The book contains valuable information about …

- Stress
- Change
- Egos
- Mentors
- Health
- Attitude
- Criticism
- Achievement

- Communication
- Technology
- Expectations
- Leadership
- Enthusiasm
- Laughter
- Salesmanship
- The Power of Praise

The book also contains 86 great examples of people being TURKEYS! In a world full of turkeys, this book is *Essential Reading* for anyone who seeks success!

Just go to our website, **www.RobertStevenson.org**, and click on our online store to purchase the book.

Beyond Excellence

One of Mr. Stevenson's most requested programs on DVD.

This fast-paced program is filled with advice on how to become an extraordinary person in business and in life. Using real world examples, dozens of slides, and powerful true stories, Robert Stevenson delivers a high-energy program that can help anyone to achieve higher levels of excellence.

He covers a broad spectrum of ideas, including leadership, accountability, dealing with stress, handling change, how to handle criticism, the power of laughter, how to exceed expectations, achieving a well-balanced life, and much more.

Whether you are just starting out in business or a seasoned professional, these ideas will remind you of all the things you need to do when you are committed to soaring above and beyond excellence.

Just go to our website, **www.RobertStevenson.org**, and click on our online store to purchase the DVD.

Free Articles From Mr. Stevenson

Mr. Stevenson writes a piece entitled **"Consider This"** for his clients that he would be happy to share with you. There is no charge, and all you have to do is send us an e-mail at ...

info@robertstevenson.org

and type, *"please add me to your e-mail list,"* (along with giving us your name) and we will take care of the rest.

He shares these thoughts with you because he believes they will be valuable, informative, interesting, or useful.

ABOUT THE AUTHOR

Robert Stevenson is one of the most widely recognized speakers in the world and the author of the best-selling book, *How to Soar Like an Eagle in a World Full of Turkeys*. He is a man who is consistently honored with standing ovations and requests to bring him back next year. As a highly sought-after speaker, he addresses audiences more than 100 times per year throughout the world. He knows for his audiences to understand, retain, and act on what he has said, he must carefully blend humor, facts, inspiration, conviction, and audience participation. This is where he excels.

His client list reads like a Who's Who in business. Companies like FedEx, Prudential, Lockheed Martin, Time Warner, Anheuser-Busch, Chevron, American Express, and Blue Cross Blue Shield continue to rely on him for a fresh, unique perspective on businesses' most crucial issues. He has shared the podium with such renowned professionals as Tom Peters, former President George H. W. Bush, former Secretary of State Colin Powell, General Norman Schwarzkopf, Anthony Robbins, and Stephen Covey.

Mr. Stevenson is a man who has lived his experiences, not just studied them. He has held positions from Salesman to Chief Executive Officer. His ability to connect with his audiences is amazing, be it a strategic planning session for a Fortune 500 company to 20,000 salespeople in a convention center. He knows how to deal with risks, competition, and the ever-changing technology in the business arena. He is known for the incredible amount of research he puts into each speech. He has interviewed over 10,000 employees, managers, and senior executives in over 200 different industries and delivered over 2,000 speeches specifically customized to meet his clients' needs. If you are interested in having Mr. Stevenson address your organization or want to receive information about one or more of his programs, please contact us at:

Email: info@robertstevenson.org
Tel: (727) 789 – 2727

We will be happy to provide you with a complete media package that will include program descriptions, fees, scheduling, and transportation requirements, along with a video demo disc, or you can go directly to his website for all of this information. We look forward to hearing from you.

www.robertstevenson.org